USING THE LIBRARY

Troll Associates

USING THE LIBRARY

by Laurence Santrey

Illustrated by Bob Dole

Troll Associates

Library of Congress Cataloging in Publication Data

Santrey, Laurence.
   Using the library.

    Summary: Explains how to find books on all subjects in
the public library's collections.
    1. Libraries—Juvenile literature. 2. Public libraries
—Juvenile literature. [1. Libraries. 2. Books and
reading] I. Dole, Bob, ill. II. Title.
Z665.5.S26   1984   025.5'874   84-2590
ISBN 0-8167-0122-9 (lib. bdg.)
ISBN 0-8167-0123-7 (pbk.)

It's possible to travel through time and space without going anywhere. All it takes is a book. Books can carry you back to ancient Rome or drop you right into the middle of a strange garden on a distant planet.

Books can teach you how to build things, how to speak a foreign language, or how to care for a pet. Books can introduce you to famous people. They can make you laugh or cry. And they can give you the past, present, and the future.

There are books on every subject imaginable. In fact, there are more books than anyone could possibly own. That is why we have public libraries for the whole community to use. Each library is a treasure house of information and pleasurable reading. It's all there, waiting for you, if you know how to use the library.

You can become a member of your public library as soon as you write your name on a library card. Then, when you want to borrow books to read at home, you show your card to a librarian at the circulation desk. The circulation desk is usually near the library's front door. This is where books are checked out and returned.

In most libraries, books may be borrowed for two weeks at a time. But every library has its own rules. Libraries also have penalties for when books are kept past the date they are due to be returned. A library usually charges a small fee for every day the book is overdue. This fine is paid when the book is returned to the circulation desk.

Not far from the circulation desk there is often a row of cabinets with small drawers. These cabinets contain the library's card catalog. The card catalog is an important tool for using the library. All the books in the library are listed in three different ways in the card catalog—by the author's name, by the title of the book, and by the subject.

Suppose a student happened to be doing a report on games of the American Indians. If that student did not know the *title* of a book about Indian games, or the name of an *author* who had written a book about Indian games, then he or she would simply look up the *subject*.

Books on Indian games might be listed under the subject GAMES or under INDIANS in the card catalog. The card for each book would show where that book would be located in the library.

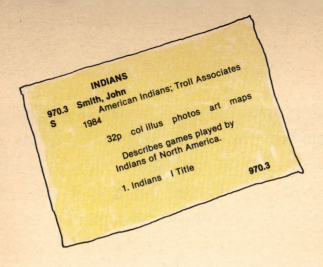

INDIANS
970.3 Smith, John
S   American Indians; Troll Associates
         1984

             32p col illus photos art maps

         Describes games played by
         Indians of North America.

             1. Indians   I Title   970.3

The card catalog is arranged in alphabetical order, from A to Z. So it is easy to find the right drawer of cards. In addition, there are guide cards in each drawer. The guide cards stick up a little higher than the other cards. On the guide cards there may be single letters of the alphabet, parts of words, or whole words. Guide cards can help you by guiding you to the right place in the drawer.

Each card in the card catalog shows the author and title of a book. It shows who published the book and the year it was published. The card also shows how many pages the book has and if it is illustrated with photos, artwork, or maps. In addition, the card has an *annotation*, which is a brief description of the book's subject matter.

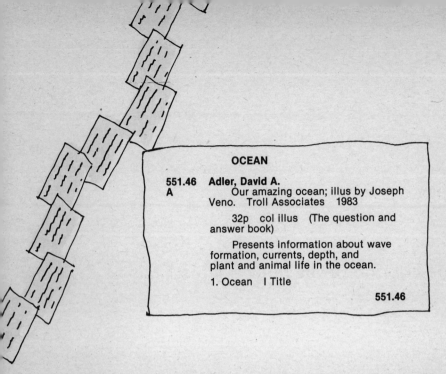

OCEAN

551.46 **Adler, David A.**
A   Our amazing ocean; illus by Joseph
         Veno. Troll Associates   1983

            32p col illus (The question and
         answer book)

            Presents information about wave
         formation, currents, depth, and
         plant and animal life in the ocean.

         1. Ocean   I Title

                                      551.46

The call numbers usually appear in the upper left-hand corner of the card. These numbers and letters tell where in the library the book can be found.

Works of fiction, such as novels and storybooks, are arranged in a special fiction section of the library. There, they are placed alphabetically by the first letters of the author's last name. For example, the books of Louisa May Alcott come before the books of Joseph Altschuler, because A-L-C—as in ALCOTT—comes before A-L-T—as in ALTSCHULER.

Nonfiction books are usually arranged according to the Dewey decimal system. This system is named after Melvil Dewey, who created this method of classifying library books.

The Dewey decimal system is divided into ten main divisions. These are divided in turn, into smaller sections and subsections. It is a simple, logical way to classify books on any and all subjects.

Dewey Decimal System

100	Philosophy and Psychology
200	Religion
300	Social Sciences
400	Language
500	Science
600	Applied Science
700	The Arts
800	Literature
900	History, Geography, Biography
000	General Works

Books on philosophy and psychology are numbered from 100 to 199. Books on religion are numbered from 200 to 299. The books in the 300s are about social sciences, such as communication and transportation. The books in the 400s are about languages, and include dictionaries.

Science is found in the 500s. Applied science and useful arts, such as aviation and pet care, are in the 600s. Books in the 700s deal with music, art, and sports. In the 800s, literature, including poetry and plays, is found. History, geography, and biography are all classified in the 900s.

The numbers 0 through 99 are assigned to encyclopedias and other reference books. These reference books also have a capital R in front of the number. In most libraries, reference books cannot be borrowed for home use. They are usually kept at a special reference desk, which may be supervised by a librarian.

All the other nonfiction books are kept in the *stacks*, or library bookcases. Each stack usually has a card posted, showing the Dewey decimal numbers of the books in that stack.

For instance, a card may read: 520–560. This means that the books in that stack have the call numbers 520 through 560. The number of each book is marked on the book's spine. The call number on the spine matches the call number in the card catalog —so you can find any book you want quickly and easily.

When you open a library book, the first thing you see is the part called the front matter, which includes the title page. The title page tells the title of the book, the name of the author, or—if the book contains a collection of works written by a number of people—the editor's name. There may also be the name of an illustrator on the title page. The publisher's name and the copyright information may also appear on the title page, or on the back of the title page.

A copyright on a book is like a patent on an invention. Nobody may reprint parts of any book without permission from the copyright owner.

The date of the copyright can be useful to someone doing research. Suppose you are writing a report on modern aviation. In that case, you want to read recently published books, because you wouldn't get up-to-date information from a book written many years ago. A copyright date is an indication of how recent the book's information is.

There are other kinds of front matter in most nonfiction books. The preface, or foreword, is a section that gives a short description of the book's purpose. The table of contents is an outline of the book's divisions, called sections and chapters.

A glance at the table of contents can often show you whether the book contains what you are looking for. A list of illustrations, as well as an introduction, may also be found in the front matter. The introduction may be a general description of the book, or it may tell about the book's author.

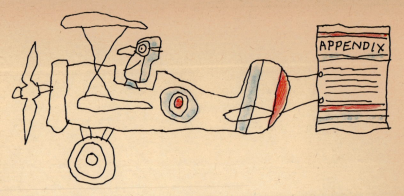

At the back of a nonfiction book is the back matter, which may include an appendix, a bibliography, a glossary, and an index. An appendix may contain charts, maps, graphs, and other material to aid in understanding the text.

The bibliography is a listing of books and articles the author consulted in preparing the book. Sometimes there is also a list of books a reader might want to get for further information on the same subject.

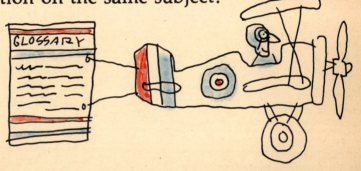

A glossary is a word list with definitions. It contains difficult, unusual, or foreign words used in the book. The index, printed in alphabetical order, is probably the most important part of a book's back matter. The index is a list of names, places, subjects, and other key elements of the book. By looking at the index, you can tell if the book has the material you need and on what pages it can be found.

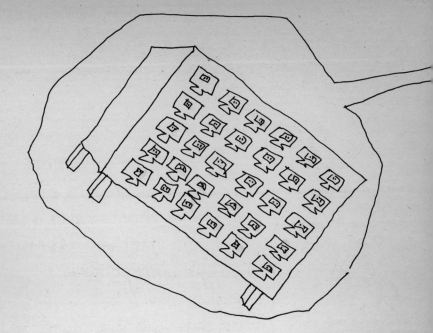

A person can learn a great deal from books and from using the library. At first, the library may seem like a huge mystery. But don't be scared away by that. Just ask the librarian for help. That's the librarian's job—to answer any question you may ask about books, facts, words, or ideas.

If you don't know where to find a reference book, how to use the card catalog, how to borrow a book, or how to get one that isn't in the library, ask a librarian. There's nothing a librarian enjoys more than sharing the treasures of the library.

Books are just one of the treasures in modern libraries. Many have sections for magazines and newspapers, some of which are recorded on microfilm. You may look at the microfilm on special viewing machines.

Libraries also have phonograph records and tapes. And there are filmstrips and movies. Some libraries even lend paintings and statues, puppets and puzzles, games and projects. The library is, indeed, a rich source of learning and pleasure—and one that you may use for the rest of your life.